DECISION TO LOVE

Bert Ghezzi and Peter Williamson
General Editors

Decision to Love

What It Means to
Love Others from the Heart

Ken Wilson

Servant Books
Ann Arbor, Michigan

Published by Servant Books
P.O. Box 8617
Ann Arbor, Michigan 48107

Cover Photo: John B. Leidy,
© copyright 1980 Servant Publications

Scripture quotations are taken from the *Revised Standard Version*, copyright 1946, 1953, © 1971, 1973 by the Division of Christian Education of the National Council of the Churches of Christ in the U.S.A.

Printed in the United States of America

ISBN 0-89283-086-7

Contents

Living as a Christian

In human terms, it is not easy to decide to follow Jesus Christ and to live our lives as Christians. Jesus requires that we surrender our selves to him, relinquish our aspirations for our lives, and submit our will to God. Men and women have never been able to do this easily; if we could, we wouldn't need a savior.

Once we accept the invitation and decide to follow Jesus, a new set of obstacles and problems assert themselves. We find that we are often ignorant about what God wants of us as his sons and daughters. For example, what does it mean practically to obey the first commandment — to love God with our whole mind, heart, and strength? How can we know God's will? How do we love people we don't like? How does being a Christian affect what we do with our time and money? What does it mean "to turn the other cheek?" In these areas — and many others — it is not easy to understand exactly what God wants.

Even when we do know what God wants, it can be quite difficult to apply his teaching to our daily lives. Questions abound. How do we find time to pray regularly? How do we repair a relationship with someone we have wronged or who has wronged us? How do we handle unruly emotional reactions? These are examples of perplexing questions about the application of Christian teaching to our daily lives.

Furthermore, we soon discover that Christians have

enemies — the devil outside and the flesh within. Satan tempts us to sin; our inner urges welcome the temptation, and we find our will to resist steadily eroding.

Finally, we must overcome the world. We are trying to live in an environment that is hostile toward what Christians believe and how they live and friendly toward those who believe and do the opposite. The world in which we live works on our Christian resolve in many subtle ways. How much easier it is to think and act like those around us! How do we persevere?

There is a two-fold answer to these questions: To live successfully as Christians, we need both grace and wisdom. Both are freely available from the Lord to those who seek him.

As Christians we live by grace. The very life of God works in us as we try to understand God's teaching, apply it to our lives, and overcome the forces that would turn us aside from our chosen path. We never stand in need of grace. It is always there. The Lord is with us always, and the supply of his grace is inexhaustible.

Yet grace works with wisdom. Christians must *learn* a great deal about how to live according to God's will. We must study God's word in scripture, listen to Christian teaching, and reflect on our own experience and the experience of others. Many Christians today lack this kind of wisdom. This is the need which the *Living as a Christian* series is designed to meet.

The book you are reading is part of a series of books intended to help Christians apply the teaching of scripture to their lives. The authors of *Living as a Christian* books are pastoral leaders who have given this teaching in programs of Christian formation in various Christian communities. The teaching has stood the test of time. It has already helped many people grow as faithful servants of the Lord. We decided it was time to make this teaching available in book form.

All the *Living as a Christian* books seek to meet the following criteria:

- **Biblical.** The teaching is rooted in scripture. The authors and editors maintain that scripture is the word of God, and that it ought to determine what Christians believe and how they live.

- **Practical.** The purpose of the series is to offer down-to-earth advice about living as a Christian.

- **Relevant.** The teaching is aimed at the needs we encounter in our daily lives — at home, in school, on the job, in our day-to-day relationships.

- **Brief and Readable.** We have designed the series for busy people from a wide variety of backgrounds. Each of the authors presents profound Christian truths as simply and clearly as possible, and illustrates those truths by examples drawn from personal experience.

- **Integrated.** The books in the series comprise a unified curriculum on Christian living. They do not present differing views, but rather they take a consistent approach.

The format of the series makes it suitable for both individual and group use. The books in *Living as a*

Christian can be used in such group settings as Sunday school classes, adult education programs, prayer groups, classes for teen-agers, women's groups, and as a supplement to Bible study.

The *Living as a Christian* series is divided into several sets of books, each devoted to a different aspect of Christian living. These sets include books on Christian maturity, emotions in the Christian life, the fruit of the Holy Spirit, Christian personal relationships, Christian service, and very likely, on other topics as well.

This book, *Decision to Love,* is part of a set of books which communicates essential Christian wisdom for maturing in Christ. To grow in living the Christian life, we must learn about faith, love of God, love of neighbor, and our identity as sons and daughters of God, to name just a few topics. To reach spiritual maturity, Christians must know how God enables us to overcome the obstacles that inevitably arise: our own wrongdoing, the power of the world, the flesh, and the devil. *Decision to Love* and other books in this set present practical, scripturally based teaching that will help you attain basic maturity in your Christian life.

The editors dedicate the *Living as a Christian* series to Christian men and women everywhere who have counted the cost and decided to follow Jesus Christ as his disciples.

Bert Ghezzi and Peter Williamson
General Editors

Preface

What is love? The first time one of my children asked the question, my answer was downright weak. It went something like this: "Love? Well, it's similar to liking someone, only much more . . . It's the feeling you have for special people . . . Actually it's hard to explain, but you'll catch on."

At the time, I took some comfort in the fact that many others were in a muddle over love. Everyone was for it, but few seemed to know precisely what it was. Widely divergent perspectives on love, ranging from naive enthusiasm ("What the World Needs Now, Is Love, Sweet Love"— Hal David and Burt Bacharach) to confirmed cynicism ("If two people love each other there can be no happy end to it"— Ernest Hemingway), only compounded the general confusion.

In the midst of the muddle, the teaching of Jesus is clear: no love, no Christianity. This unavoidable conclusion is motivation enough to learn what Christian love is and put it into practice.

The Lord doesn't want us to be confused by conflicting perspectives on love; he wants us to have his perspective. And he doesn't want our understanding of love to be vague or confused. He wants to teach us what Christian love is.

God had a straightforward strategy for bringing his love, Christian love, into practice. First, he put love at the very heart of Jesus' message. Second, he revealed the nature of love through Jesus' words and example. Third, he poured out upon his disciples the power of his Spirit to love. And fourth, he provided practical teaching about how love should work in a variety of relationships. God's strategy is effective. When Christians

— put love at the heart of their Christianity,
— understand the nature of Christian love,
— rely on God's power as the source of love, and
— follow the teaching of scripture on the application of love in various relationships,

they are able to love as Jesus did.

But there is a hitch. Because we hear so much about love, we may simply assume that we know what Christian love is. Dulled by the thought that we've heard it before, we may pass over some of the most radical teaching in the New Testament. Or assuming that we know what love is, we may fail to question popular notions of love, lumping these in with the Christian ideal.

To understand what Christian love is and to put it into practice requires nothing less than the kind of transformation that Paul wrote about in his letter to the Romans: "Do not be conformed to this world, but be transformed by the renewal of your minds" (Rom 12:2). Over the years, I've had to change my mind considerably about what Christian love is. I've discovered that Christian love, like God himself, is often much different that we might think.

commandment. And a second is like it, You shall love your neighbor as yourself. On these two commandments depend all the law and the prophets" (Mt 22:37-40). Jesus showed us that these two great commandments are inextricably bound together. And, by linking the second commandment so closely to the first, Jesus made loving others a matter of central importance. Together these commandments form the core of all genuine Christian life.

All too often we lose this focus and concentrate on other things. For example, Christians who have experienced renewed faith through the gifts of the Holy Spirit can forget that the main point of their lives does not revolve around experiencing gifts and having spiritual experiences, but rather on loving others. The Apostle Paul, who faced just this problem with some young Christians in Corinth, says, "If I speak in the tongues of men and of angels, but have not love, I am a noisy gong" (1 Cor 13:1). Others, who are rightly convinced of the need for sound doctrine, may see orthodoxy as the one mark of Christianity, forgetting that the fruit of the Spirit is love. Elsewhere Paul writes, "Knowledge puffs up, but love builds up" (1 Cor 8:1).

Some of us are simply impatient when it comes to learning about something as basic as love. Our thinking goes something like this: "No doubt we shouldn't forget about love, but when are we going to get down to some of the deeper truths, something we can really sink our teeth into? " I've heard comments like this more than once, and each time I respond with stronger conviction. When will we learn something more weighty than love? Never.

John couldn't have said it more plainly: "He who does not love does not know God; for God is love" (1 Jn 4:8). Understanding more complicated or subtle truths may give us a sense of satisfaction, a sense that we are growing in spiritual maturity. But love is the most profound truth because love is at the center of God's being. One can't penetrate more deeply than that.

Jesus himself addressed the problem of misplaced priorities. After answering the Pharisee's question about the greatest commandment, he denounced them for ignoring the more important matters of the law: "You blind guides," he said "straining out a gnat and swallowing a camel!" (Mt 23:24). Our most important priorities are to love God and our neighbor. To multiply the lesser things to make up for a lack of the greater just won't do.

Summary

To understand what Christian love is and how it should operate, we must first see the importance that God places on it. Though love is one of the Christian basics, it is not something just for beginners. We grow into it, not out of it.

TWO

What Is It Anyway?

Inexperienced hunters have an unnerving tendency to shoot at anything that moves. The dangers of this approach are obvious. The first commandment for hunters is: "Know your prey and don't shoot—or even take aim—if you are not sure that what you have in sight is what you want to kill." Neglecting this important rule might only result in some wasted ammunition, but it might also lead to the loss of a good hunting dog or worse yet, another hunter. Eagerness without understanding is no virtue.

The Christian who is eager to practice Christian love must know what he is aiming for. This is of special concern these days when there is so much confusion about the nature of Christian love. The question is not "Love— pro or con? " but rather, "How should we understand and express love? " It is absolutely crucial to distinguish between the Christian conception of love and the ideas that most people have about love. These ideas are often very different, and Christians should recognize the differences. Otherwise, we may make love our highest priority, only to find that we are pursuing something that isn't really Christian love at all.

For example, many of us think of love primarily as a feeling. We think that we are loving someone when we have positive feelings for them. If the emotional response is missing, we may conclude that love is missing too. Is this particular view of love the same as Christian love? No. Such a view is certainly not a scriptural view. Scripture, for the most part, speaks of love in different terms.

Many people equate love with feeling, but that doesn't mean that Christians ought to adopt this view. Very often popular notions about love will not coincide with the Christian perspective. Today, Christians face the challenge of understanding what Christian love is and what it isn't.

In the midst of the confusion, God has given us his word to rely on. By examining the biblical teaching on love we can see how it contrasts with various popular conceptions.

Christian Love Is Service Love

Now before the feast of the Passover, when Jesus knew that his hour had come to depart out of this world to the Father, having loved his own who were in the world, he loved them to the end. And during supper, when the devil had already put it into the heart of Judas Iscariot, Simon's son, to betray him, Jesus, knowing that the Father had given all things into his hands, and that he had come from God and was going to God, rose from supper, laid aside his garments, and girded himself with a towel. Then he poured wa-

ter into a basin, and began to wash the disciples'
feet, and to wipe them with the towel with which
he was girded (Jn 13:1-5).

John introduces this section of scripture by saying that Jesus "loved them to the end." Then, as
an example of Jesus' love, he describes what must
have been a most unusual event. In Jesus' day, foot
washing was a task reserved for the youngest servant or slave. Here was Jesus, the master, taking the
position of a lowly servant, performing an act of
common service. By washing the disciples' feet
Jesus, in effect, defined love in terms of service.

We should remember that this was not a merely
ceremonial act. The feet that Jesus washed were the
sandaled feet of men who had spent most of the day
walking along crowded, dusty roads. In all likeli-
hood, they were very dirty feet. And Jesus took a
towel and a basin of water and washed them.

When he had finished this act of service, Jesus
told them, "If I then, your Lord and Teacher, have
washed your feet, you also ought to wash one
another's feet. For I have given you an example,
that you also should do as I have done to you" (Jn
13:14-15). Later that night he added, "A new commandment I give to you, that you love one another;
even as I have loved you, that you also love one
another" (Jn 13:34).

Jesus served his disciples by washing their feet,
and in so doing he loved them. Christian love is
service love. It includes a wide range of actions,
from the everyday to the heroic, but the point is
this: when we serve others, we are in fact loving

them; we are practicing Christian love.

A few years ago, my wife seriously strained her back. The doctor prescribed the only remedy available: three weeks of lying on the floor without doing any work. This was simple enough except for the fact that our children were still in need of much supervision, and I couldn't leave my job for three weeks to pick up the slack.

At first my wife just assumed that the remedy was worse than the malady. But we made a few phone calls to ask some of the members of the Christian community that we are part of to help us out. A number of people volunteered to come to our house to do whatever we needed: to cook, clean, care for the children, and so on. For three straight weeks, a small group of Christians served us in this way. Even though we weren't especially close to a number of them, one thing I know: in serving my family, they were practicing Christian love.

Service love can be expressed in extraordinary, even herioc acts, but very often it involves everyday, ordinary expressions. Listening attentively to a co-worker's problem, helping a neighbor fix his car, making a husband's lunch (five days a week for twenty years) can all be expressions of the love Jesus exemplified when he washed the disciples' feet. It is the kind of love practiced without fanfare, day after day.

Another aspect of service love— sometimes so obvious that we fail to recognize it— is the simple fact that it is something we *do*. It is expressed in deeds, whether small or great. In this sense it involves much more than simply "being nice" or having a positive disposition or intention.

Imagine that you are planning to move from one house to another and have asked several of your friends to help out. They all generously agree to lend a hand. But when moving day arrives, only one person shows up. When you call the others, they all have excuses of one sort or another. Some have forgotten, others "can't get free," but they all insist that they want to help— as if to say, "it's the thought that counts." Of course in this situation, the thought didn't really count for much. You were looking for help, not best wishes.

When we understand that love is service to others, we see that Christian love has to be practiced if it is to work.

A Vanishing Perspective

In 1977 a large conference on Christian unity was held in Kansas City. A friend of mine was a volunteer worker. His job was to assist one of the conference leaders however he could. My friend introduced himself to the leader by saying, "I'm here to help you in whatever way I can — make phone calls for you, run personal errands, deliver messages, anything that would make it easier for you to carry out your responsibilities. Just think of me as your personal servant during the conference." The leader protested, "No, I couldn't do that; there's no servant class in the kingdom; we're all brothers." The leader was obviously ill at ease with the prospect of allowing my friend to serve him. Not that he didn't trust him or think that he could do a good job;

he simply wasn't used to the idea of service. The fact is, service is a vanishing dimension of our society and our personal relationships. We are not used to it, and we don't value it.

The men whose feet Christ washed had a different experience of service than modern-day disciples have. To them, service was a familiar aspect of their relationships. As children, they were trained to serve their parents; as those who were learning a trade, they served the one whose apprentice they were; as young men, they served their elders; and as disciples, they served their master.

Jesus took what was for them a commonly experienced aspect of human relationships and showed them how it was to be applied in his kingdom. His application was often new (for example, the idea that leadership is a service, not a matter of "lording it over" others), but at least he was teaching men who were used to serving others.

When it comes to our personal relationships— with family, friends, neighbors, and co-workers— we aren't nearly as comfortable with the idea of serving as the disciples were. Somehow it doesn't seem fitting or dignified.

Once I saw a girl pick up some items that belonged to her brother; she was helping him get ready for a trip. A neighbor standing nearby told her, "Don't be his slave; let him carry his own things." The message was clear: don't lower yourself to serve your brother; it isn't fitting.

The teaching of scripture, though, is different. We ought to be eager to serve others— even in menial, unpleasant ways. For us, service has been dignified by the example of Jesus. It is an important part of loving others.

Christian Love Is Putting Others First

"This is my commandment, that you love one another as I have loved you. Greater love has no man than this, that a man lay down his life for his friends" (Jn 15:12-13).

By nature, Christian love is ready for self-denial, even the kind of self-sacrifice that Jesus performed by laying down his life. In fact, according to Jesus, love's highest expression is the laying down of a man's life for his friends. This ideal of self-sacrifice, expressed in everyday terms, means putting others first— placing our concern for others above our concern for ourselves.

Some time ago, Gale Sayers, a professional football player, wrote a book called *I Am Third* (God first, others second, myself third). It stands in refreshing contrast to a bestseller called *Looking Out For Number One*. The latter title reflects a trend in contemporary thought that is becoming increasingly popular. This view of life goes something like this: I'm "number one"; I should consider others' needs only inasmuch as they further my own goals, or to the extent that I shouldn't infringe on their basic rights. According to this book, love is and ought to be selfish. Selflessness is regarded as disguised selfishness.

As this view of life becomes more popular, it can

become easy for Christians to be influenced by it. The aim of love becomes increasingly self-centered. Concern for self takes on a more "honest," positive connotation, while selflessness is viewed with greater suspicion. When faced with this perspective, we ought to examine the assumptions that lie behind this view of life. Robert Ringer, the author of *Looking Out For Number One*, acknowledges his indebtedness to Ayn Rand for many of his views. Several times he refers to her book entitled *The Virtue of Selfishness*. As the title indicates, this book exalts the ideal of selfishness and rejects as naive— and even dangerous— the ideal of putting others first. Rand's view of the world places man at the center of all things. There is no god other than oneself. Putting self first is merely the appropriate response to this reality.

Christians see things differently. I am not the center of all things. I am not even the center of my own life. God is. Apart from God, the principle of selfishness holds true for me— my behavior will be dominated by self-interest. But in the new creation, things work differently. I draw my life from Jesus, and his way of loving is not based on self-interest. "Have this mind among yourselves," wrote St. Paul, "which is yours in Christ Jesus, who, though he was in the form of God, did not count equality with God a thing to be grasped, but emptied himself" (Phil 2:5-7). Rather than exalting the self, Christian love is patterned on the example of Jesus, who emptied himself. Jesus put others before himself and instructed his followers not only to receive the benefits of his self-sacrifice but to do likewise.

Granted, putting others first can be bothersome. The principle has very practical and costly applications. Time and money are good examples. If I have some money and give it to you, I've expressed Christian love. I also have less money than I had before. Or if I have a certain amount of free time that I spend on serving others, it is no longer available for personal use. There's just no getting around the fact that sometimes Christian love hurts!

Never Say No?

To say that we ought to serve others, to put them first, is not to say that we should never turn down opportunities to serve. I mention this because many of us find it hard to say no. But "no" is not a four letter word. Sometimes we won't be able to do what others want us to do and sometimes we shouldn't, even if we are able.

One women I know, Beth, was a receptionist for a Christian organization. When staff members of the organization called the office, they would often pass on little projects for "someone" to take care of. Since Beth answered the phone, she received more than her share of such requests. And even though it was appropriate to turn down some of these requests in order to do more important things, Beth found this extremely hard to do. "If I'm supposed to be loving these people," she wondered, "how can I turn them down?" Beth mistakenly assumed that love means never saying no. We shouldn't pretend that we don't have limits. We do. And that means that sometimes we will have to turn down legitimate requests.

There are other times when we must say no. A friend of mine was a bank manager. One of the loan procedures seemed to deceive customers about the actual cost of the loan. My friend's boss wanted him to overlook the problem, but my friend told him that he couldn't comply with his wishes. There are times like this when our actions ought to displease others. Love doesn't dictate that we please everyone all of the time.

Similarly, being a loving person doesn't mean that we have to be a "nice guy." A nice guy is someone who doesn't rock the boat; he never gets angry, and he doesn't get involved in confrontations.

Sometimes rocking the boat or confronting someone is the most loving thing to do. Suppose that a friend of yours, who is in some financial bind, has asked you to look over his income tax forms. As you review his returns, looking for ways that he can save money, you notice that he is cheating.

You want to love him and you want to be nice to him. What do you do? Do you confront him with his dishonesty and risk offending him, or do you keep quiet and pray that he doesn't get caught? In this case, love dictates that you call him on it— better you than the IRS. To take the nice guy approach, though it would keep things smooth and comfortable, would not really be loving your friend.

The love of Jesus wasn't contentious but neither was it afraid of conflict. Jesus loved Peter, but when Peter insisted that Jesus turn back from his last journey to Jerusalem, Jesus chose some tough words to address his friend: "Get behind me Satan." He wouldn't let Peter advise him on a course of action that was different from what he knew to be his Father's will.

Summary

To understand what Christian love is, we must also understand what it is not. Our view of love should be a Christian view, regardless of what others think. By its very nature Christian love involves service. When we serve others we are in fact loving them. Christian love means putting others first; it involves self-denial and self-sacrifice. The Christian ideal flies in the face of a growing contemporary mentality that places concern for one's self as the highest goal. This mistaken view has nothing to do with the teaching and example of Jesus.

Sometimes Christians equate putting others first with a timid, "never-say-no" approach. Or they think that being a loving person means being a "nice guy" all the time. Because we have limits, we will sometimes have to turn down legitimate requests. Sometimes righteousness may require a negative response. There are also occasions when it's right to express anger or to confront someone. To avoid these in order to be a "nice guy" would be a failure to love.

THREE

If Not Feelings, Then What?

If asked what lies behind the love one has for a spouse, for family members, or for a close friend, many people would point to a feeling of sexual attraction or of personal affection and warmth. At first glance, this shouldn't surprise us. The positive feelings that we sometimes call "love" are an important aspect of our close relationships. But Christian love, though it normally involves our feelings, is not *based* on feelings. Christian love is based on commitment.

If we view love primarily as a feeling we can run into some real problems. For one thing, our emotions don't provide the most solid foundation on which to base our relationships. We have some control over our feelings— often much more than we think— but for the most part we can't simply pick and choose them. Some days we feel good and some days we feel bad. At times the reasons are clear, while at other times our feelings are hard to explain. A foundation like this is shaky ground indeed.

Just how shaky this kind of foundation is can be seen in the case of romantic love. Songs that glorify the love between a man and a woman also portray it as a love that comes and goes. It seems that it is outside of our control. On any popular radio station, one is likely to hear of love's ups and downs in rapid succession. The first title asserts with confidence, "I Believe There's Nothing Stronger Than Our Love" while a second proclaims, "Love Will Keep Us Together." But a third is likely to tell us of a love gone cold: "You've Lost That Lovin' Feelin'." While the disc jockey might philosophize "Well, that's love for you," our conclusion ought to be just the opposite: whatever it is, it isn't love.

If this is what the New Testament means by love, how could Jesus command it? In fact, the basis of Christian love is not a feeling but a commitment to serve, to put others before ourselves. We can decide to commit ourselves to others; we can choose to love.

Thus, in Christian marriage, love is not based on a feeling, but on a commitment to love and serve the other person. For this reason, the marriage vows stress the fact that love will weather good times and bad.

Unfortunately, many husbands and wives today don't understand the strong foundation that Christian love really is. Rather than rooting love in a personal commitment, they base it on feelings of mutual attraction.

The story of the play "Camelot" is a good example of this. King Arthur marries the Lady Guinevere. They seem to be a pretty good match and to live happily until Arthur invites Sir Lancelot to join his new order of knights. Lancelot and Guinevere fall in love— they exchange telling glances, notice one another across rooms full of people, and so on. But rather than recognize what is really going on— that they are developing a romantic attraction to each other— they conclude that this is "true love," true enough to justify breaking a marriage covenant and betraying a friendship. The play idealizes this view of love. It is not that Lancelot and Guinevere are caught in their own weakness. To deny their romantic attraction would involve a breach of integrity. They have no choice; they must be true to love.

If we approach love from this angle, it can have disastrous results. Ed and Louise are a fictitious couple, but their story— a modern-day Camelot— represents the kind of thing that happens all too often. Ed and Louise were married after graduation from college. Their view of love tended to focus on the positive feelings they had for each other, feelings that during a couple of years of dating remained strong and fairly steady. They thought that if they kept in touch with their feelings and maintained good communication, their marriage would succeed. The first few years of their marriage went well. But then Louise began to experience some confusion about the direction her life was taking; she became increasingly dissatisfied with her career and with the prospect of having children. All this began to influence her feelings for Ed. Disagreements that were ordinarily resolved or easily forgotten became exaggerated out of all proportions. Before too long, Louise reached a decision: as hard as it was to face it, she had fallen out of love with Ed. She felt that the only honest thing to do was to end the marriage. Though Ed didn't feel the same way, neither did he want to keep the marriage together if Louise's "heart wasn't in it." They parted good friends, but they parted. After that, neither Ed nor Louise had much confidence that future relationships would last any longer.

Things should work differently for Christians. In a Christian marriage, love is the commitment that the partners make— to "have and to hold, for better or worse, for richer, for poorer, in sickness and in health till death parts us." Anyone married for longer than a month knows that feelings toward your spouse can vary, depending on a long list of factors. But husband and wife are committed to serve each other, to "lay down their lives" for each other, to love each other— with or without the help of feelings.

The point is not that feelings are unimportant but that emotions in a good marriage are clearly subordinate to marital love, to the personal commitment that each partner makes to the other. The commitment doesn't depend on positive emotions, and it isn't destroyed by negative emotions.

Because Christian love is a commitment, God can and does hold a husband and a wife responsible for whether or not they love one another. Christian love can survive even when both partners are not experiencing the normal positive feelings toward each other.

What is true of the love between husband and wife in a Christian marriage is true of our love for other people as well as our love for God. Our emotional attraction can and, in many cases, will waver, but our love can remain constant. On a graph it might look like this:

Time

When I became a Christian, I experienced several feelings. For one, I felt as though I were returning home after a long time. This feeling helped me to give my life to God. It also assured me that I was doing the right thing. But I also had a feeling of fear— not the fear of being in God's holy presence, but the nagging fear that maybe I was making a big mistake. That feeling didn't help very much. I had to ignore it.

Since then, my love for God— my commitment to serve him, to put him first, to obey his commandments— has been made either easier or more difficult by various feelings. When I'm feeling good, it seems easier to love God; when I'm feeling low, it's more difficult. But either way, I'm commited to loving him. Over time I've noticed that my feelings are generally more positive, and I've also noticed that how well I love God is much less influenced by negative feelings.

Christians who equate love for God with their

feelings toward God are apt to evaluate their relationship with him on the basis of how they feel. This often results in a downward spiral of introspection and emotional gymnastics. We can imagine a scene that may not be uncommon. An unsuspecting Christian wakes up early one morning in order to pray before he goes to work. He puts a slice of bread in the toaster and turns on the radio, hoping to catch the latest weather report. Just then, when his defenses are down, the song I mentioned earlier comes on the radio: "You've Lost That Lovin' Feelin.'"

The hauntingly melancholic tune is followed by the weather report: a steady drizzle throughout the day.

With the mood of the day thus set, our faithful, but by now somewhat gloomy Christian finishes breakfast and goes to pray. He begins his prayer time by reading a chapter from the book of Revelation: "Fortitude you have...But I have this against you: you have lost your first love. Think from what height you have fallen— repent! "

He stops reading. The song on the radio runs through his mind. Then the thought comes to him: "You don't love God anymore— where are those feelings you used to have for God? Gone! "

There is no need for us to create our own "dark night of the soul" by evaluating our love for God by the feelings we have. A more accurate standard is committed love. Are we putting God first? Are we seeking to serve him? Are we loyal to him and his ways? If we are growing in these areas, we are growing in our love for God, whether or not we feel positively toward God at a particular moment.

Love from the Heart

We often hear that love ought to be "from the heart." In other words, love ought to be authentic, sincere, without pretense. To say that we can love someone even when we don't have positive feelings toward them may seem contrary to this ideal.

The apparent contradiction stems from the way we think about the heart. Most often, we tend to equate the heart with feelings. In scripture, as well as in contemporary usage, the heart is a symbol for the center of who we are. From our hearts our attitudes and behavior spring. "As in water face reflects face, so the heart of man reflects man" (Prv 27:19). God can influence us on a number of levels, but if he can get to our hearts, he's gotten to *us*. Love from the heart, therefore, is love that flows from the center of who we are. Now if we say that the heart is synonymous with the emotions, then we would have to conclude that love cannot be authentic without positive feelings. But the ancient Hebrew understanding of the heart is quite different. The heart was seen as the place of fundamental choice. A heart commitment was understood as a commitment that was intelligent and decisive as well as something that involved the feelings.

When a modern man wants to know who someone really is, what he is really like, he tries to understand what the person is feeling. He might ask, "Tell me what you feel about what I just said — on the 'gut level,'" meaning on the level of feelings.

Many of the modern approaches to communication, lay a heavy emphasis on articulating one's feelings. We can hear one another saying, not "I think thus and so," but "I feel thus and so."

But the scriptural view of the heart is not so lopsided. In addition to the feelings, the heart includes intelligent thought and decision. To love one another, as St. Peter enjoins, "earnestly, from the heart" means that we make a commitment to one another at the level of fundamental choice. It is a commitment that involves thought and decision, as well as feelings. In his letter to the Romans, Paul wrote, "God's love has been poured into our hearts through the Holy Spirit which has been given to us" (Rom 5:5). When God pours his love into our hearts, he has chosen to influence us on a level deeper than the emotions. His influence reaches us at the most fundamental level. Because God has poured his love into our hearts, we are free to make a decisive commitment to love. This love will normally involve our feelings, but it will not depend on them.

Commitment Can Lead Where Feelings Won't Go

We can authentically, sincerely, honestly love someone from the heart even on those occasions when our feelings don't support our commitment to love. If you think of your feelings as representing the "real you" then you will consider it hypocritical to love someone when you don't have the corresponding feelings. But because the heart exists at a more fundamental level than the emotions themselves, Christian love is love from the heart even when the feelings don't cooperate.

Before I understood the difference between love and feeling, I spent considerable energy in unnecessary soul searching. My thoughts would go something like this: "I may be doing all the right things to love so and so, but am I really loving him? If I really loved him, I'd want to be with him all the time, and I wouldn't have these negative feelings that I occasionally experience. How long can I maintain this sham that I call love? What kind of hypocrite am I, anyway? "

When someone explained to me the true meaning of Christian love, something clicked. It was a great relief to realize that I didn't need to strive to have positive feelings at all times toward those I loved. In fact, simply seeing this helped me to have more positive feelings toward people who "rubbed me the wrong way." I was like the man who finally realized that the worst way to start up a conversation is to say, "Now let's have a good conversation." I found that the feelings worked better when the focus was off them.

Now I can have deeply committed relationships with those whom I am not naturally attracted to. A friend of mine, Joe, is an example. When I first met him, it was obvious to me that we would never become friends by the natural selection process that determines most friendships. I didn't especially like him.

We had very little in common. Joe was an engineer; I studiously avoided the sciences. Joe was a master of details, not one of my strong points. His ethnic background was hotblooded, mine, cool and reserved. His sense of humor and mine were completely different.

If I had relied on my natural inclinations to establish a committed relationship with Joe, it never would have happened. But I found that my commitment to love him as a brother in Christ allowed me to learn to like him as a friend. The commitment came first and the natural inclination followed.

The same principle is illustrated by the experience of a mother I know who has three children. Ann told me that after the birth of her third child, she became concerned when the usual feelings of affection were, for one reason or another, absent. She felt altogether neutral toward her newborn child. When Ann discussed the matter with her husband, he encouraged her to continue to love the child believing that sooner or later the feelings would follow.

It turned out to be good advice. The situation didn't change overnight— in fact, it took a few months before Ann was experiencing the more normal feelings that a mother has for her child. But rather than condemning herself for three months (for "not loving her own child") Ann simply continued to love the child, expecting her feelings to come around.

Because Ann knew that she could love her baby without the feelings that are normally present, she was spared considerable grief and confusion. Ann didn't worry about her lack of feelings. She continued to care for the child; she expressed a mother's warmth and affection for the child even as she was waiting for her feelings to develop.

Committed Not Cold

In order to illustrate the fact that love is primarily a commitment, not a feeling, we have described various situations in which love survived when feelings could not. But this does not mean that commitment and feelings are opposed to each other. By no means! Our emotions are given to us by God to help us follow and serve him and to help us love one another.

Christian love shouldn't be dry, cold, calculated and emotionless— "I'll love you because I'm a Christian, but I'll be darned if I'll like you." Christian love is warm, personal, and affectionate. It includes our feelings.

C.S. Lewis described the relationship between committed love and what he called the natural affections by using the analogy of a garden. Natural love, with its feelings, spontaneous friendships, and so on, is like an untended garden that grows beautifully at times, but also tends to run wild or dry up. Our feelings are like a lush growth within us, beautiful when the conditions are right, but apt to overgrow in some places and not to grow in others. When we exercise Christian love, we are like the gardener who removes weeds, trims overgrowth, and plants and transplants according to his design for the garden. He keeps the garden from turning into a jungle or drying up in the middle of a drought. The ideal is not love devoid of feeling. Instead, our commitment is the basis for love and provides the context for natural affections. Love built on the foundation of commitment will normally flourish and involve positive feelings. It will be warm, pervasive, and personal. It will be like a fruitful garden.

When I was introduced to members of the Christian community that I am now part of, I was impressed by the natural warmth and affection they expressed for one another. People frequently greeted each other with a hug; their speech was encouraging and positive; and they didn't "cut each other down" with humor. Coming from a more reserved family background, all this warmth was, to be honest, a bit much. Since I was used to a cooler way of expressing love, my first reaction was suspicion: "It can't be genuine." When I eventually joined our community, I thought that I might succeed in reinstituting the handshake as the primary form of greeting. My attempt failed miserably. The more I realized that all this warmth and affection was backed by personal commitment, the more I appreciated the value in openly and personally expressing love. As I learned to receive expressions of affection more graciously, I was also able to express my love for others in a more personal way. I learned to appreciate that God's love for me was closer to the warm affectionate brand than the cool and understated variety.

Summary

The foundation for Christian love is commitment, not feeling. Though feelings are often involved in love, positive feelings are not required for love to exist. The popular, romantic view of love, particularly as it is portrayed through the media, often equates love and feelings. When the feelings sour, love sours. A marriage based on this foundation is headed for trouble. In a Christian marriage, love is the commitment that each partner makes to love and serve the other. A marriage based on committed love can survive even when feelings don't support this commitment. Committed love is love "from the heart." Since the heart is the place of fundamental choice, committed love involves intelligent thought and decision, as well as feelings. Though Christian love doesn't depend on feelings, neither is it cold, calculated, or impersonal. Christian love ought to be warm, expressive, and affectionate.

FOUR

No Strings Attached

G.K. Chesterton said that the chief object of education is not to learn things but to unlearn things. We've needed to unlearn much about love in order to understand what Christian love is. Unlearning will be no less significant in understanding that Christian love is unconditional.

Recently I heard about some marriage ceremonies that make the conditions of love very explicit. Instead of promises to love "in sickness and in health, for richer for poorer, till death parts us," these vows were something like this:

"I promise to love you as long as I can remain true to myself as a human being."
"I promise to love you as long as we are able to facilitate each other's highest potential."
"I. promise to love you as long as our love remains."

These vows express a commitment, but it is a conditional commitment. It is good only as long as the condition is met.

Christian love is unconditional. Our natural inclination, though, is to attach conditions to our love. These conditions constitute forms of love that we must unlearn.

Selective Love

We are naturally inclined to love only those who are like us. Whether the selection is along racial, common interest, psychological, occupational, or economic lines, it involves the addition of a condition. "I'll love you as long as you _____." Each of us could fill in the blank with a different set of conditions.

Many modern men and women are highly selective about whom they will love. A typical pattern involves choosing two or three close friends and ignoring nearly everyone else. As the numbers decrease the conditions increase. Such friends are chosen because they are highly compatible. Possible sources of conflict are thereby minimized to get the most out of the relationships.

This was the pattern I followed before I was a Christian. I had two close friends. These relationships formed a tightly knit circle that had several good aspects. But it was basically a closed circle. Highly committed relationships were limited to that small group.

Eventually the three of us became Christians and joined the same community. Close ties still exist between us (in many ways the ties are closer because of our Christian commitment), but now we are each close to a number of other people, and we are highly committed to a wide variety of people who are not at all like us.

Profitable Love

Love your enemies, do good to those who hate you, bless those who curse you, pray for those who abuse you. . . . If you love those who love you, what credit is that to you? For even sinners love those who love them. And if you do good to those who do good to you, what credit is that to you? For even sinners do the same. And if you lend to those from whom you hope to receive, what credit is that to you? Even sinners lend to sinners to receive as much again. But love your enemies, and do good, and lend, expecting nothing in return; and your reward will be great, and you will be sons of the Most High; for he is kind to the ungrateful and the selfish (Lk 6:27-28, 32-35).

Christian love doesn't require a return on the investment. Our natural tendency is to love only those who are able to love us in return, or those who appreciate us. But that doesn't take Christian love to the limit. When Jesus commanded us to love our enemies, he set a higher limit on love.

No doubt there will always be people who we have difficulty loving. This is normal. Some may be our enemies— people who for one reason or another want to harm us— but most will be the kind of people who just "rub us the wrong way." Sometimes the only profit in loving these people whose personalities clash with our own is the profit that comes from the "sand-paper effect." This occurs when the irritating qualities of another produce something needed in us— greater patience, tolerance, flexibility, and so on. It is a form of divine polishing. Though we can benefit from this polishing, it doesn't provide the primary motivation for loving others. We are called to love others, regardless of whether we profit from loving them.

At times, these hard-to-love people will appreciate our efforts. But even when they don't we are to love and serve them, just as Jesus did.

> Now on his way to Jerusalem, Jesus traveled along the border between Samaria and Galilee. As he was going into a village, ten men who had leprosy met him. They stood at a distance and called out in a loud voice, "Jesus, Master, have pity on us."
>
> When he saw them, he said, "Go, show yourselves to the priests." And as they went, they were cleansed.
>
> One of them, when he saw he was healed, came back, praising God in a loud voice. He threw himself at Jesus' feet and thanked him— and he was a Samaritan.
>
> Jesus asked, "Were not all ten cleansed? Where are the other nine? Was no one found to return and give praise to God except this foreigner? " (Lk 17:11-18).

Though Jesus did not approve of ingratitude—

in fact, he spoke against it—his love was not contingent upon returned thanks. When we find ourselves serving those who don't remember to express appreciation, our response should not be, "That's the last time I do anything for them." Like our master, we should expect to love and serve those who are not thankful. A pastor I know calls this our "ministry to the ungrateful." It is a service that cannot be performed with the kind of love that depends on profit.

Christian love may, at times, be profitable. Love has an infectious quality. Those whom we love will tend to return love. But the personal profit is not our concern. We are to love whether there seems to be a profit or a loss.

Guarded Love

"Love is risky business. What happens if the person you love turns around and betrays you? What happens if the person dies, or meets some personal tragedy? Doesn't love just set you up for getting hurt?" Guarded love tries to protect itself from injury. The avoidance of pain, difficulty, and trial then becomes a condition attached to love.

This approach to relationships is becoming increasingly common as people experience the skitterish quality of the kind of love that is based on feelings.

Frank became a Christian a few months after his divorce had been finalized. He was enthusiastic about his new relationship with God, but when it came to getting to know other Christians he was reluctant. Frank was outgoing and personable, but after a while those who were in close contact with him realized that they didn't know him very well.

I spent some time trying to get to know Frank better. One day I asked him directly: "Why is it that you keep your relationships on a superficial level?" Frank then told me about his relationship with his ex-wife and the divorce. During the divorce proceedings he made a vow never to let himself get close to another person. Love was too unpredictable, and he just wasn't cut out for its ups and downs. Even as a Christian, Frank was cynical about the possibility of sustaining loving relationships. He was plagued by two thoughts. Perhaps it was all a sham. Maybe these brotherly relationships only *seemed* different than the shaky relationships he had developed in the past. Or perhaps he was really incapable of sustaining committed relationships.

Of course Christian love is not guaranteed to be painless. Christians are still capable of sinning and hurting one another. St. James said that love "covers a multitude of sins," implying that there would be plenty of sins to cover. Enduring relationships are made possible by *enduring* injury though committed love, not by avoiding injury.

Rather than devising elaborate defense systems, the Christian can take a different approach to handling injury in personal relationships. One of the first things taught in self-defense courses is the right way to fall. Instructors are realistic; they assume that their students will sustain a good kick or two. Knowing how to fall, or how to "roll with the punches," is an important skill.

Christians too can learn how to sustain injury in personal relationships— through forgiveness, forbearance, handling conflict directly, and so on— without tightening up, or maintaining a guarded distance.

Self-Fulfillment Love

"I need to have love relationships in order to be fulfilled." Who would reject this as a statement of fact? We all need love relationships in order to be fulfilled. The problem is not with the idea of self-fulfillment in itself, but in viewing self-fulfillment as a goal of life.

When self-fulfillment is the ultimate goal, the tendency is to look at love relationships as a means to achieve the goal. Too often, this approach leads us to focus on my need for love or my fulfillment through love. A contribution to self-fulfillment then becomes just another condition to be met.

The Christian's goal is not self-fulfillment, but the love of God and neighbor. The scriptures encourage a focus on others, not self. We love, not in order to fulfill a personal need, but in response to God's love: "We love, because he first loved us" (1 Jn 4:19). Love is not the means to the higher end of self-fulfillment, happiness, or personal satisfaction. Love is the end.

Behavior Modification Love

Experimental psychologists have discovered just how effective the age-old techniques of reward and punishment are for changing behavior. Using these techniques, rats, for example, can be trained to accomplish surprisingly complicated exercises. An enterprising class of undergraduate students was even reported to have used these techniques on their psychology professor. As he moved to the corner of the room and leaned on one leg, they acted especially attentive. When he moved away from the spot or stood on both legs, they acted bored. Before long, their professor lectured from the corner of the room, leaning on one leg.

Because love is so powerful, we are tempted to use it as a reward, or its withdrawal as punishment. But that is a conditional form of love. Christian love is not to be used in this way.

This means that we don't withdraw our commitment to love another person, in order to punish him for something he did wrong, nor do we threaten to withdraw our love in an effort to motivate him to change.

In other words, love or the promise of more love, shouldn't be used like a carrot stick. My son tried this on me once. He said, "Dad, if you take me out for ice cream, I'll love you even more." I refused the offer. After all, that kind of love wouldn't outlast the ice cream.

I don't want to give the impression that we are acting inconsistently if we love others and at the same time try to change them. We can accept others and love them at the same time we try to modify their behavior. God's acceptance and love for us is a good example of how this can work in our relationships with each other.

At most of the Billy Graham evangelistic rallies, Graham invites those who want to make a commitment to Christ to gather round the speaker's podium. As the people stream down from their seats, a famous hymn is sung, "Just as I am...O Lamb of God, I come." The words of the hymn express an important truth: God invites us to come to Jesus for salvation whatever our condition. The Christian message is not "change, then come" but "come as you are." Nonetheless, change is part of the package. "Come as you are, but don't stay as you are; be transformed into the likeness of Christ."

The point about behavior modification love is that love shouldn't depend on behavior, not that we should never try to modify someone's behavior. In fact, there are times when we are obligated to try to change the way another person acts. For example, when a child misbehaves it is up to his parents to see that his behavior changes. We shouldn't neglect our responsibility (when we actually have that responsibility) to help or even insist that someone change. But we shouldn't threaten to stop loving them if they don't change.

Parity Charity

Parity charity is concerned with keeping things even. During my first few years of marriage, I had parity charity developed to a quantifiable science! Of course, that's an exaggeration, but I did tend to keep track of small and large acts of kindness on some imaginary ledger. If I thought that I was behind, I would exert energy to perform some good deeds in order to keep things even— to maintain an equal distribution of love. The whole approach led to frustration. Either I was behind (and feeling vaguely guilty) or ahead (and feeling like I was on the short end of the stick). The quest for parity was like the quest for the unreachable star.

Eventually I came to understand that Paul's advice to husbands, "Love your wives, as Christ loved the church" (Eph 5:25), disqualified parity charity. I couldn't imagine the Lord approaching his church that way, and I was certainly thankful that he had not applied that principle to me.

Many married couples find themselves lodged in a parity charity deadlock. By each partner's assessment the other is lagging behind. So each waits for the other to even the scales. Only unconditional love— love that isn't concerned about unequal distribution— can break the deadlock.

Marriage isn't the only context in which parity charity is practiced. One can relate to the sum of all one's relationships on that basis: "I'm always giving but never receiving," or "I'll never be able to return all the love I'm receiving." Of course our assessment is often inaccurate. But the fact that we so often misjudge how well the scales are balanced isn't the only problem with parity charity. At times, the scales *are* objectively out of balance; there are times, for example when we are clearly giving more than we are receiving. Either way, it doesn't matter. As John wrote, "We love, because he first loved us" not "we love to keep things even."

In whatever guise it appears, conditional love is not Christian love. Christian love is based on God's unconditional love for us, the kind of love that reached out to us even when we were God's enemies. "Once you were alienated from God and were enemies in your minds because of your evil behavior. But now he has reconciled you by Christ's physical body through death to present you holy in his sight, without blemish and free from accusation" (Col 1:21-22).

Summary

The love practiced by Christians should be unconditional. Our natural inclination, however, is to attach conditions to our love for others. Conditional love comes in many forms. Selective love would have us only love those who are like us. Profitable love urges us to love only when we can see that our investment will yield a return. Guarded love seeks to protect us from injury or disappointment. Self-fulfillment love places our need for fulfillment above everything. Behavior modification love uses love as a reward or punishment to change someone's behavior. Parity charity attempts to keep things even, never giving more or less than the other person. These are all distorted forms of love. Christian love, like God's love, is unconditional.

FIVE

The Source

If we understand the nature of Christian love and our own human limitations, we will readily conclude: Christian love is impossible. In one sense that's true. Any merely human effort to practice Christian love will inevitably fall short and will likely lead to exhaustion or a redefinition of Christian love that seems more manageable.

In fact, the sooner we realize our limitations, the better. It will make it easier for us to rely on God for the power to practice Christian love.

During World War II a woman named Corrie ten Boom found herself in a situation that compelled her to depend on God's power to love. Her family, living in Holland, hid Jews from the Nazis. When they were discovered, Corrie and her sister, along with other family members, were sent to a concentration camp. For Corrie the hardest part was watching how the atrocities of the camp affected her sister, who eventually died in prison. Everything within her wanted to hate the Nazi soldiers. And who would have blamed her?

In fact, Corrie experienced a tremendous struggle not to hate those men. She realized that she could love them only if God provided the love. She had faith that God wouldn't call her to love her enemies if he didn't provide a supernatural source of love. By relying on the Lord as her resource, she was able to love the Nazi soldiers.

Loving with God's Power

Without the power of God's Spirit, Christian love is just another unreachable goal: lovely to behold but impossible to attain. The Holy Spirit provides us with the power to practice Christian love. As Paul says, "God's love has been poured into our hearts through the Holy Spirit which has been given to us" (Rom 5:5).

Love didn't originate with us. We can't manufacture it. It comes from God alone. God's Spirit within us provides this love, making God's own love available to us. When we practice Christian love, we're drawing on the power of God, through the action of the Holy Spirit.

A friend of mine used to act very disrespectfully toward his parents. He would argue with them, ignore them, and yell at them. Even when he resolved to act lovingly toward his parents, he found that he simply couldn't. He was powerless to alter his behavior.

His relationship with his parents was one of the first things that changed after he came to know Jesus and receive the power of his Spirit. His behavior altered radically; he was able to love them, to treat them respectfully, and care for them. In fact

the change was so remarkable that it inspired his
mother to commit her life to Christ.

It Takes Faith

In order to practice Christian love, we need to
rely on the power of God. It is a matter of faith. We
love because we are commanded to love. And he
who requires love also provides it through his Holy
Spirit, which has been given to us. If we refuse to
believe this, it will be very difficult for us to actually
receive God's power to love; like everything else in
the Christian life, it comes through faith.

Quite often, love flows freely from us because the
Holy Spirit lives within us. It is a natural effect of
our relationship with the Lord, something of which
we may not even be conscious. A friend of mine,
after recommitting his life to the Lord and praying
to be filled with the Spirit, was asked if he noticed
anything different about his life. At first he drew a
blank; nothing especially dramatic or noteworthy
seemed to be different. Then he said, "Come to
think of it, I do seem to love people a lot more than
I used to. I don't think that I'm working any harder
at loving others— it's just happening." Because my
friend was putting his faith in the Lord and learning
to live in the Holy Spirit, his capacity for love increased.

But sooner or later, we will all run into situations
where love doesn't seem to be flowing freely.
Sometimes we are challenged by the circumstances,
as Corrie ten Boom was when she was faced with
the prospect of loving her captors. Or we may be
challenged by obstacles within ourselves: old preju-

dices, emotional problems, and the like. When this happens, we will need to exercise faith in a more specific, active, and aggressive way. When we find ourselves unable to love as we ought, there are several things we should do.

1. *Ask God for help.* If you find that you are having difficulty loving a particular person, don't simply try harder. Ask God in specific terms for the help that you need. "Lord, give me the power that I need to not be irritable with Jane. Help me to have your perspective on loving her; enable me to love her today." If need be, keep on asking. Don't give up after one or two feeble requests.

2. *Expect your prayer to be answered.* Jesus said, "Therefore I tell you, whatever you ask in prayer, believe that you have received it, and it will be yours" (Mk 11:24). The Lord wants us to exercise expectant faith. We can always pray with the highest level of confidence for the power to love.

3. *Stop pressuring yourself.* Your energy ought to be directed toward having faith that God will give you the power you need, and away from pressuring yourself to do better. Sometimes it is difficult to distinguish between pressuring yourself and simply deciding to love the person in spite of the obstacles. The former doesn't usually help while the latter is often necessary. The best way to tell the difference is to consider the focus. Self-pressure is usually focused on the problem: how big and terrible it is. It is also focused on yourself: how you really ought to be able to love this person and how miserably you are failing. Self-pressure does not focus on God's ability and faithfulness to help, on his prom-

ise to provide for our lack. The spirit behind this type of pressure is nagging rather than encouraging.

4. *Do the loving thing.* The faith approach is not passive or effortless. When Peter was invited to step out of his boat and walk toward Jesus, who was himself walking on the water, he had to *do* something. He had to swing his legs over the side of the boat, set his foot on the waves, and begin to walk. Peter took a literal step of faith. The same kind of faith is needed when it comes to loving those we find hard to love. Faced with such a challenge, begin to behave in a loving way toward the person. Look for opportunities to help him or her, to say something kind or encouraging, to *do* something that will express love. Praying for the other person can be one such expression. Don't just pray that God will make them more lovable or remove their irritating habits; pray for the person's welfare, for an increased measure of God's blessing. At any rate, don't rely on your feelings to motivate you, and don't balk at doing the loving thing just because you don't have positive feelings for the person. Your feelings are more likely to change *after* you start behaving in a loving way.

A friend's experience illustrates how this can work. Rick and his wife were living in an apartment building. The downstairs neighbor was a young woman who held frequent, large, and loud parties. Bothered by the noise, Rick became quite irritated with his neighbor. This was a difficult person for him to love. One day Rick sensed that the Lord wanted him to love the woman in spite of her behavior. He asked the Lord to help him, and later that day he had some ideas about what to do. He was still irritated by the parties and his feelings about the woman were not very positive, but he decided to implement some of his ideas anyway. He and his wife had the woman over for dinner. He made a point to offer his help if she ever needed it. Both he and his wife did some concrete things to express love for her. After this, Rick began to see this woman from a different perspective— as someone who needed God's love, and not simply as a source of irritation. He still didn't like the noisy parties downstairs, and he continued to insist that the woman quiet things down, but this did not keep him from loving her.

Summary

If we think that Christian love is impossible, we are on the right track. Apart from the power of God working in us, it is. But because God's Spirit has been poured into our hearts, we can love others as Jesus did. But it doesn't happen without faith. Our need to exercise faith in the power of God is most evident when we are finding it difficult to love someone, for whatever reason. Rather than struggling on our own, we should take a faith-filled approach. We should ask for God's help with the confidence that he is able to provide what we lack. We should stop pressuring ourselves and concentrate instead on God's promise. Finally, we should "step out" in faith and begin to do the loving thing, even if our feelings don't support us.

SIX

Respecting the Differences

When I first began to understand that Christian love was unconditional, a fear took shape in the back of my mind. I would imagine myself walking down the street having just cashed my paycheck. A panhandler would ask for some money, and I would give him my week's wages, returning to my family empty-handed.

Now this particular fear isn't entirely illogical. For a family man to give his paycheck to a panhandler would be an expression of his unconditional love for the panhandler. We have no guarantee that God would never ask us to do such a thing. But though it is important to see that Christian love is unconditional, we should also see that love is not indiscriminate. We are to practice Christian love in all relationships, but we are to express it differently in various kinds of relationships.

Types of Relationships

The scriptures make clear distinctions between different types of relationships and provide instructions for how to behave in these relationships. The

following list covers many of the different relationships referred to in scripture:

> God and man
> husband and wife
> brothers and sisters
> brothers and sisters in Christ
> elders and members of communities
> civil authorities and citizens
> masters and slaves
> parents and children
> rabbi and disciples
> host and guests
> enemies
> "outsiders" (non-Christians)

Much of the wisdom of scripture concerns itself
with what these various relationships should look
like and what God expects of us in the relationships.
Though there is much overlap, there are also differences in the instructions given for each relationship. The scriptures also indicate the kind of priority that each of the relationships should have. For
example, the fact that the parent-child relationship
is addressed specifically in the Ten Commandments
— "Honor your father and your mother" — says
something about the importance that God places on
that relationship.

This has important ramifications for our discus-
sion on love since Christian love is not practiced in
a vacuum, but in the different personal relationships in which we are all involved. Christian love
does not ignore the variations among relationships;

it respects them. To practice Christian love effectively we have to practice it differently, depending on the relationship.

Biblical Greek is better equipped than English to capture the various expressions of love. The writers of the New Testament use different Greek words to distinguish between sexual love, brotherly love, familial love, and hospitable love. All these types of love can be expressions of "agape," the Greek word the authors of the New Testament chose to describe Christian service love.

Next, we'll consider the biblical approach to the love of fellow Christians, the love of outsiders, and the love of guests.

Love of Brothers and Sisters

Having purified your souls by your obedience to the truth for a sincere love of the brethern, love one another earnestly from the heart (1 Pt 1:22).

So then, as we have opportunity, let us do good to all men, and especially to those who are of the household of faith (Gal 6:10).

"A new commandment I give to you, that you love one another, even as I have loved you, that you also love one another. By this shall all men know that you are my disciples, if you have love for one another" (Jn 13:34-35).

The "love of the brethren" (or those who are of

the "household of faith") is the special love that Christians should have for each other. It is a specific form of Christian love, reserved for a particular relationship.

In recent times, the idea of Christian brotherhood has been confused with what is called the brotherhood of man. This latter term refers to our common creation by God, our common dignity as human beings, our common nature as members of the human race, our common call by God to obey him, and our common responsibility to treat one another justly. But the brotherhood of man is not a scriptural term; and neither is it synonymous with Christian brotherhood as described in the Bible. The New Testament does teach that we are to love all men, including our enemies. But when the New Testament refers to "brothers" or "the brethren" it refers to those who share in a covenant relationship with God and one another. We become brothers and sisters in this sense, not simply by being born into the human race, but by believing in Jesus and receiving power to become children of God.

A Family Relationship

Brothers and sisters in Christ are members of the same spiritual family. When Peter asked the Lord what was in store for those who left all to follow him, Jesus said, "There is no one who has left houses or brothers or sisters or mother or father or children or lands, for my sake and for the gospel, who will not receive a hundredfold now in this time, houses and brothers and sisters and mothers and children and lands, with persecutions, and in the age to come eternal life" (Mk 10:29-30).

One of the women in our community had the unique experience of growing up with five brothers and then raising six sons. She used to think that sisters and daughters just weren't part of God's plan for her life. Then she came into the kind of family relationships that exists between members of our community. She realized that God was more than making up for her lack. She literally had hundreds of sisters, many of whom were young enough to be her daughters.

Christians are not merely associates or colleagues or common interest holders. The bond that exists between Christians is a family bond.

Family, Not Clique

Because the love of the brethren does not include everyone, it can be viewed with suspicion, or mistaken as cliquish. In fact, the relationship that ought to exist among Christians is a family relationship rather than an elite relationship. We wouldn't consider a family to be a clique because they ate dinner together or had a special relationship. On the contrary, we would admire a family in which members had strong bonds of loyalty and commitment to one another.

Christians are part of the same family, not the same clique. The same bonds that hold the natural family together are required to hold the church together. The same lack of commitment that threatens the natural family threatens relationships between Christians.

This is not to say that Christian groups never act like cliques. Sometimes they do. When members of a Christian group find themselves behaving like members of an exclusive elite— when they become smug, or relate condescendingly to outsiders, or fail to welcome newcomers— they ought to stop acting like that. They ought to repent. But they shouldn't stop practicing the love of the brothers or weaken their commitment to each other or try to pretend that they don't have a special relationship as fellow Christians.

A Yardstick

There is no need for Christians to be apologetic about their special love for other Christians. Scripture places a high priority on this kind of love and we should too. In fact, the scriptures view the love of the brethern as a yardstick; it is a measure of a person's Christianity. St. John speaks of it as one of the signs that a person is living in Christ. "If we love one another, God abides in us and his love is perfected in us" (1 Jn 4:12).

It is one of the indicators that we have passed from death to life. "We know that we have passed out of death into life, because we love the brethren" (1 Jn 3:14).

The Love of Outsiders

But God, who is rich in mercy, for the great love he bore for us, brought us to life in Christ even when we were dead in our sins; it is by grace you are saved...There is nothing for anyone to boast of. For we are God's handiwork, created in Christ Jesus to devote ourselves to the good deeds for which God has designed us.

Remember then your former condition...you were at that time separate from Christ, strangers to the community of Israel, outside God's covenants and the promise that goes with them. Your world was a world without hope and without God. But now in union with Christ Jesus you who were once far off have been brought near (Eph 2:4-5, 9-13).

The New Testament gives more detailed instructions about how we ought to love outsiders, but this passage provides a helpful perspective by showing us that we were all at one time "outsiders." More than that, the scriptures are careful to remind us that the fact that we belong to God is nothing that we can claim credit for. It is a matter of unmerited favor; because we have earned nothing, we have nothing to boast of.

The man who helped me commit my life to the Lord had not forgotten his former condition. As an agnostic, I was sometimes frustrated by his confidence. It was clear that he knew he had something that I didn't. But I never got the impression that he was better than I, even though I envied his position as a Christian. He wasn't shocked by my values when they were contrary to Christian values. And he wasn't surprised when I did things that he considered wrong. He knew that I was under a different ruler, living by different rules. Though he didn't accept my way of life as a good way to live, he seemed to understand it. This was one reason that he gained my trust and why his words about Jesus had such an influence on me.

Here then are a few of the more specific instructions about our love for those who are not Christian:

> Maintain good conduct among the Gentiles, so that in case they speak against you as wrongdoers, they may see your good deeds and glorify God on the day of visitation (1 Pt 2:12).

> Conduct yourselves wisely toward outsiders, making the most of the time. Let your speech always be gracious, seasoned with salt (Col 4:5-6).

> Honor all men. Love the brotherhood. Fear God. Honor the emperor (1 Pt 2:17).

> For what have I to do with judging outsiders? Is it not those inside the church whom you are to judge? God judges those outside (1 Cor 5:12-13).

> If possible, so far as it depends upon you, live peaceably with all (Rom 12:18).

The New Testament's teaching about our love for those who are not Christians ("outsiders" or "Gentiles") emphasizes several dimensions.

Respect

"Honor all men." Our respect for others ought to overcome any natural tendency to look condescendingly on those whose way of life is different than ours. We ought to communicate respect both in the way that we speak about non-Christians and in the way we relate to them.

Graciousness

"Let your speech be gracious." To be gracious is not simply to be polite. Graciousness is a matter of generously extending favor to others, even when such favor isn't merited. In this we imitate our heavenly Father, as Jesus commanded us, "Be merciful, even as your Father is merciful" (Lk 6:36).

Peace

"Live at peace with all men." Just as we strive for peaceful relationships with other Christians, we ought to do whatever we can to live peaceably with others. The biblical concept of peace involves more than the lack of fighting or enmity. It includes the idea that our relationships ought to be "in order." Though some aspects of our relationships with outsiders are not under our control, we shouldn't discount problems we might have with them just because they aren't brothers in Christ.

Good Deeds

"Do good to all men." Our love ought to be expressed in actions, and not merely in speech or intention. One of the primary ways that we ought to love outsiders is by helping them, by doing things to express our love.

Concern for the Gospel

"Making the most of the time." We should remember that it is God's will for those who don't know him to draw closer to him so that they too can "glorify the Father on the day of visitation." Our relationships with those who aren't Christians ought to provide opportunities for this to happen.

This does not mean that we should love non-Christians only when we see an opportunity to speak with them about the Lord. Most people know if they are being loved as an "evangelistic prospect."

Neither should we behave in a way that is inconsistent with our convictions in an effort to be accepted by non-Christians "for the sake of the gospel." I knew a man who was convinced that, as a Christian, he shouldn't smoke marijuana. But when he was around friends and relatives who smoked marijuana, he would sometimes join in. He felt that by doing this his credibility with that group of people would be improved, and hence his effectiveness in sharing the gospel with them. That's one perspective. But another way of looking at it is to pose the question, "If one of these friends became a Christian tonight, would my behavior help them, or would it confuse them? " In other words, our behavior ought to set a good example whether or not this helps us to be accepted. Better to be respected as one who does what is right than to be accepted as "one of the guys."

Judge Not

"What have I to do with judging outsiders" (1 Cor 5:12)? In the matter of judgment, Paul made a distinction between believers and unbelievers. As an elder, he had the responsibility to make judgments within the Christian community. For example, there were those whose behavior demanded that they be expelled from the community. But Paul did not take on the responsibility of judging outsiders. He left that up to God.

In summary, when we love those who are not Christians, we do not necessarily express our love in the same way that we express it for brothers in Christ. There is considerable overlap of course, but there are also differences. If we ignore the differences, we can run into trouble.

When I first became a Christian, my inclination was to ignore the distinctions between my relationships with Christian and non-Christian friends. As I found myself able to relate more deeply with Christians, I tried to relate on this same level with my other friends. It didn't work very well.

In an effort to be honest and open with non-Christian friends, I eagerly launched into conversations about my new convictions regarding certain sensitive topics, as if I were discussing the matter with a Christian. The result was not always to draw my friends closer to the Lord. In fact, it often had the opposite effect.

The Lord wanted me to love them more, to love them better, but not necessarily in the same way that I loved fellow Christians.

Love of Guests

The New Testament also speaks about another kind of love— that which is expressed by showing hospitality. Notice what it says. "Practice hospitality ungrudgingly to one another" (1 Pt 4:9). "Remember to show hospitality. There are some, who, by so doing, have entertained angels without knowing it" (Heb 13:2).

Hospitable love, or the love of guests, is another distinct form of Christian love. The passage from Hebrews probably refers to the time when Abraham was visited by three mysterious guests— messengers of God on their way to Sodom. Abraham's treatment of his guests is a good example of hospitable love.

Abraham greeted them with respect, bowing down before them. Then he invited them into the shade of his tent and offered to wash their feet and provide refreshments. Abraham served them a fine meal; and when it came time for them to leave, he escorted them a short way down the road (Gn 18).

In the time of the New Testament the recipients of hospitality were usually Christians traveling from other cities— men like Paul and Barnabas with an itinerant ministry. They received a particular form of love from the brothers and sisters which, like

Abraham's hospitality, was expressed through specific actions. Like brotherly love or the love of outsiders, hospitable love was another distinct expression of love, reserved for a particular context (caring for guests) and expressed in a particular way.

Depending on the Relationship

Christian love is not like a standardized commodity to be expressed in the same way in all relationships. There are different expressions of Christian love for different relationships. Though the various forms of love are all Christian love, they are nonetheless distinct. Christian love cannot be practiced effectively without regard for the distinction between various relationships. For parents to express their love for their children through hospitality would be inappropriate— and exhausting. And if a father disciplined one of his guests like he disciplines his children for misbehaving, Christian love wouldn't justify his actions. Husband and wife express love through a sexual relationship, but that particular expression is misplaced in any other relationship.

In order to love well, we need wisdom about how to express love in different relationships. And wisdom to love, like power to love, must come from God. The Lord wants to give us that wisdom, wisdom for parents to love their children and children their parents, wisdom for married couples, wisdom for Christians to love one another, and wisdom to love those who aren't Christians— Godly wisdom to practice Christian love in all its expressions.

Summary

The scriptures provide wisdom about how love is to be expressed in various relationships. The love we have for fellow Christians, for example, is expressed differently than the love we have for those outside the Christian community. The love that we show toward guests represents another form of Christian love. Failure to respect the differences in various relationships leads to much confusion about love.

Conclusion

Several years ago a Lennon-McCartney song was popular. The title was "All You Need Is Love." Were the lyrics a straightforward statement about love or were they a bit cynical, rendered with a touch of mockery? Given the poorly grounded view of love in our culture, I can understand why someone might detect a hint of cynicism. What hope is there in a love built on the shifting sands of feelings or on a love that shys away from lasting commitments or on a love that is in fact "rational self-interest?" What kind of alternative is a Christian form of love that is essentially the same as the popular version, only practiced with greater religious conviction?

If Christian love is anything, it is different, because it comes from God and is founded in Christ. My goal in this book has been to describe how Christian love is distinctly Christian so that we can love more fruitfully. Chances are, we will all have plenty of opportunities to practice.

The books in the Living as a Christian Series can be used effectively in groups. To receive a free copy of the Leader's Guide to this book and the others in the series, send a stamped, self-addressed business envelope to Servant Books, Box 8617, Ann Arbor, Michigan 48107.